Little Mitchie

LET'S LOOK INSIDE AN ANT'S NEST

LET'S LOOK INSIDE: ANIMAL HOMES

TRACY VONDER BRINK

CREATING YOUNG NONFICTION READERS

Little Mitchie books spark curiosity and support early nonfiction reading for students in Grades 2-3. Designed to build vocabulary, support second language learners, and prepare readers for middle-grade content, each book includes helpful tips for parents and educators to build confidence and deepen understanding of the world.

TIPS FOR READING NONFICTION WITH BEGINNING READERS

Talk about Nonfiction

Begin by explaining that nonfiction books give us information that is true. The book will be organized around a specific topic or idea, and we may learn new facts through reading.

Look at the Parts

Most nonfiction books have helpful features. Our *Little Mitchie* titles include color photographs and graphic aids, a table of contents, a glossary, and an index. Share the purpose of these features with your reader.

Color Photos and Graphic Aids

A lot of information can be found by "reading" photos, charts, maps, and other graphic aids found within nonfiction texts. Help your reader learn more about the different ways information can be displayed.

Table of Contents

Located at the front of the book, this list shows the big ideas within the text and the page numbers where they can be found.

Glossary

Located at the back of the book, the glossary defines key words and phrases that are related to the topic. These words and phrases can be found in the text in colored type.

Index

Located at the back of the book, an index is an alphabetical list of topics and the page numbers where they can be found.

With a little help and guidance about reading nonfiction, you can feel good about introducing a young reader to the world of *Little Mitchie* nonfiction books.

Little Mitchie is an imprint of:

Mitchell Lane
PUBLISHERS

2001 SW 31st Avenue
Hallandale, FL 33009
mitchelllanepub.com

First Edition, 2027.

Author: Tracy Vonder Brink
Designer: Jen Bowers
Editor: Tricia Hoffman

Library of Congress Cataloging-in-Publication Data
Title: Let's Look Inside an Ant's Nest / by Tracy Vonder Brink

Description: Hallandale, FL :
Mitchell Lane Publishers, [2027]

Identifiers:
ISBN 979-8-89260-877-0 (library bound)
ISBN 979-8-89260-974-6 (eBook)

Library of Congress Control Number: 2026936349

PHOTO CREDITS
Shutterstock: cover, p.1 ©2022 alvarobueno, p.5 ©2020 Bogdan Vacarciuc, p.6 ©2025 Lasse Johansson, p.9 ©2012 Lefteris Papaulakis, p.10 ©Michael Pettigrew, p.11 ©2018 corlaffra, p.13 ©2020 Michael Siluk, p.14–15 ©2022 frank60, p.16 ©2012 Andrey Pavlov, p.19 ©2016 Pavel Krasensky, p.20–21 ©2023 Eko Budi Utomo, p.22 ©Lidok_L

TABLE OF CONTENTS

Chapter One

AMAZING ANTS

Have you ever watched an anthill? Hundreds of ants rush in and out. It seems like they never stop! What are they doing in there? What's life like inside an ant's nest?

HOME SWEET HOME

Ants live in a group called a colony. The largest known colony covers at least 3,700 miles (6,000 km)! But not all ants build long-lasting nests. Army ants use their own bodies to make a moving nest that carries the queen, the eggs, and the young.

An anthill is a mound of soil. Its shape helps it **absorb** the sun's heat to keep the nest warm. The nest's entrance is in the mound. Ants use the entrance to go in and out. Some nests have more than one entrance.

Chapter Two

PARTS OF AN ANT'S NEST

Ants' nests are full of underground tunnels. The tunnels bring in fresh air, and ants use them like roads to move throughout the nest. The tunnels lead to **chambers**.

HOME SWEET HOME

Ants that live underground make nests by using their **mandibles** to dig and to move soil, sticks, and rocks. Ants can carry 10 to 50 times their body weight. That's like you lifting a couch by yourself!

One chamber is for the queen. Worker ants take her eggs to a different chamber to stay until they hatch. Then, the **larvae** are moved to a nursery chamber to grow up. Other chambers are used to store food. Some chambers are toilet areas.

HOME SWEET HOME

Leafcutter ants bring bits of leaves back to the nest to make a sort of garden. They put the leaves in a chamber and chew them up so that **fungus** grows. Then, they eat the fungus!

Chapter Three

LIFE INSIDE THE NEST

An ant's nest is never completely still. Ants take hundreds of short rests during the day and night, but they rest at different times. That means some are always awake to gather food and care for the nest.

HOME SWEET HOME

Worker ants are all female. Male ants have short lives. They die after mating with a new queen.

Ants **communicate** by making **pheromones** in their bodies that other ants smell with their **antennae**. This helps them recognize each other, work together, and signal when danger is near.

HOME SWEET HOME

Foragers can look for food any time of day or night. Some kinds of ants are more active during the day, while others are busier at night.

Foragers are worker ants that leave the nest to search for food. When they find it, they lay down a pheromone trail for others to follow. Foragers bring back bits of food and drop them off in a chamber by the entrance.

Worker ants have jobs inside the nest. Some pick up food dropped off by foragers and take it to storage chambers. Others clean the nest every day by carrying out waste. Ants that work in the nursery take food to the larvae. Some take food to the queen. Soldiers guard the anthill, ready to attack. If the nest needs to grow, workers dig new tunnels and chambers.

HOME SWEET HOME

A queen starts the nest, but once workers hatch, she never leaves her chamber again. Laying eggs is her only job.

Ants are a team where everyone plays a part. They all work together to help each other survive. Now you know what's inside an ant's nest!

A LOOK INSIDE

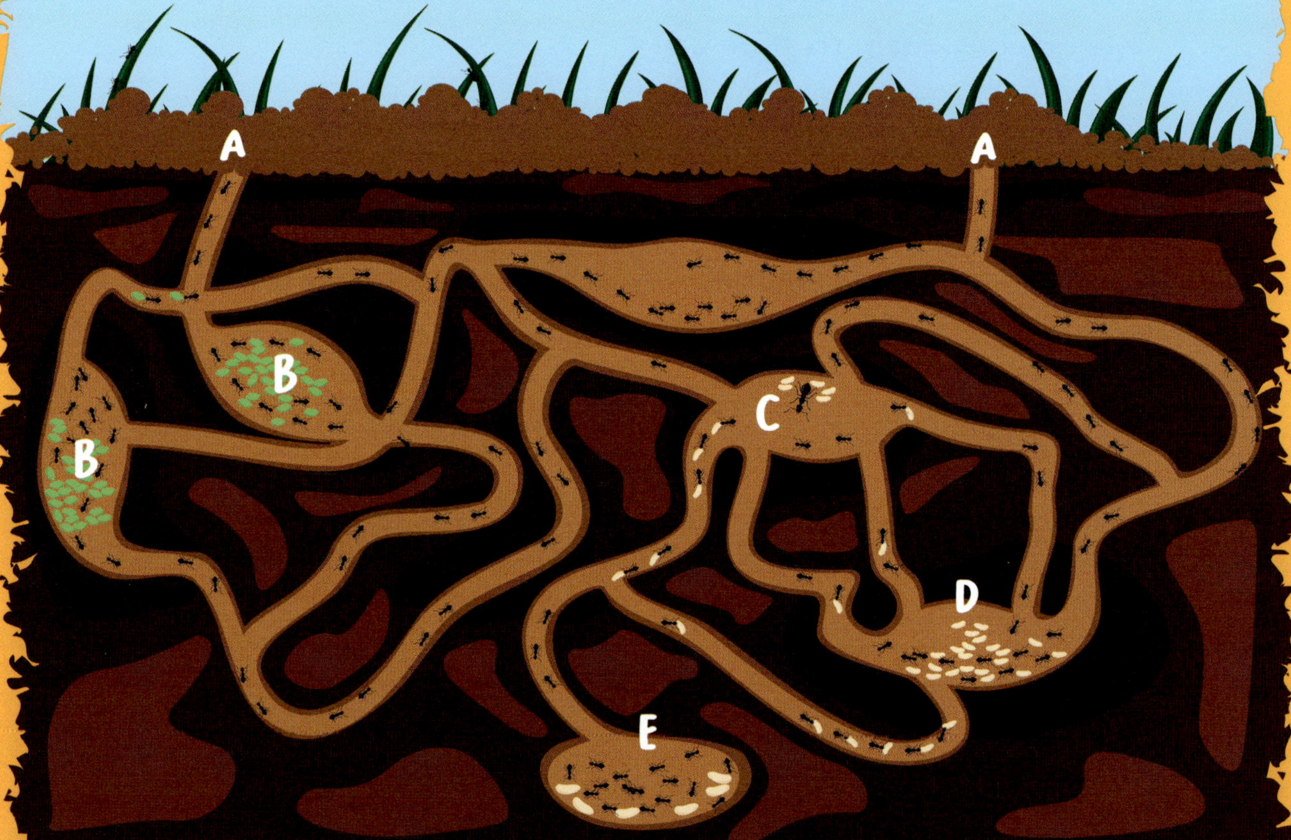

A. ENTRANCE
B. FOOD STORAGE
C. QUEEN'S CHAMBER
D. UNHATCHED EGGS
E. NURSERY FOR YOUNG

GLOSSARY

absorb (ab-zorb) to soak up

antennae (an-ten-ee) feelers on the head of an insect

chambers (chaym-burz) rooms

communicate (kuh-myoo-ni-kate) to share information, ideas, or feelings

fungus (fuhn-guhs) a plant-like organism that has no leaves, flowers, roots, or stems and grows on plants or dead things

larvae (lahr-vee) insects in the stage of development after they hatch

pheromones (fair-uh-mohnz) substances produced by animals that trigger a response in other animals of its kind

mandibles (man-duh-buhls) the biting mouthparts of some insects

FURTHER READING

Bunting, Philip. *The Wonderful Wisdom of Ants.* Crown Books for Young Readers, 2024.

DK. *Ant Antics.* DK Children, 2023.

ON THE INTERNET

10 Cools Facts About Ants!
www.natgeokids.com/uk/discover/animals/insects/ant-facts/
National Geographic Kids shares their 10 favorite ant facts.

Ants
https://kids.britannica.com/kids/article/ant/352759
Learn about ants' size, their life cycle, and more with Britannica Kids.

INDEX